Nelson Spelling

Pupil Book 1A

OXFORD
UNIVERSITY PRESS

OXFORD
UNIVERSITY PRESS

Great Clarendon Street, Oxford, OX2 6DP, United Kingdom

Oxford University Press is a department of the University of Oxford.
It furthers the University's objective of excellence in research, scholarship,
and education by publishing worldwide. Oxford is a registered trade mark
of Oxford University Press in the UK and in certain other countries

Text © John Jackman and Hilary Frost 2015
Illustrations © Marcus Cutler and Elisa Paganelli 2015

The moral rights of the author have been asserted

First published 2015

British Library Cataloguing in Publication Data

Data available

ISBN: 978-14085-2402-2

1 3 5 7 9 10 8 6 4 2

Paper used in the production of this book is a natural, recyclable product made from
wood grown in sustainable forests. The manufacturing process conforms to the
environmental regulations of the country of origin.

Printed in Italy by L.E.G.O S.p.A.

Acknowledgements
Cover illustration: Marcus Cutler
Page make-up: OKS Prepress, India

'Green Toad' from *Chronic Phonic* by Constance Milburn, included by permission
of the author.

Oxford OWL
Discover eBooks, inspirational
resources, advice and support
www.oxfordowl.co.uk

Contents

Unit 1	letters	4
Unit 2	a e i o u	6
Unit 3	sh th	8
Unit 4	ck nk	10
Unit 5	ch tch	12
Unit 6	s es	14
Unit 7	ing ed er	16
Unit 8	er est	18
Unit 9	ll ff ss zz	20
Unit 10	a-e ai ay	22
Unit 11	ee ea ie e-e	24
Unit 12	i-e ie igh y	26
Unit 13	oa o-e oe ow	28
Unit 14	oo u-e ue ew	30
	Check-up 1	32

UNIT 1

letters

a b c d e f
g h i j k l m

Key Words

ant
badger
crocodile
dog
elephant
fish
goat
horse

Focus

| a | b | c | d | e | f | g | h | i | j | k | l | m |
| n | o | p | q | r | s | t | u | v | w | x | y | z |

Look at the alphabet.
Copy the letters that come after these letters.
The first one is done to help you.

1 a _b_   2 d ___   3 r ___   4 k ___
5 b ___   6 w ___   7 s ___   8 h ___

n o p q r s t
u v w x y z

4

Extra

Which letters are missing?
Copy the letters and fill in the missing letter.

1 a __ c 2 g __ i 3 n __ p 4 r __ t

5 x __ z 6 f __ h 7 k __ m 8 d __ f

9 j k __ 10 r s __ 11 __ q r 12 __ n o

Extension

Write the first letter of these animals' names.

1

_a_ ___ ___ ___ ___

2

_k_ ___ ___ ___ ___

3

_d_ ___ ___ ___ ___

What do you notice?

Tricky Words

a   of   if   is   his   I   was   has

5

a e i o u

bug

bog

beg

big

bag

Key Words

at
cat

get
let

is
his

got
not

but
mum

Focus

Add **a, e, i, o** or **u** to make these words.
Write the words in your book.

fin   hot   cut   fan   hat   fun   cot   hit   cat

1 f___n

2 f___n

3 f___n

4 h___t

5 h___t

6 h___t

7 c___t

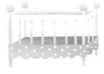

8 c___t

9 c___t

Write two words that rhyme with these words:

rat	hen	win	hot	run
hat				
bat				

Extension

A Copy this **and** pattern into your book.

and   and   and   and   and

B Look at the **and** words in the box.
Write them in your book.

sand   band   hand   land

1 s_____   2 h_____   3 l_____   4 b_____

sh
th

fish

moth

Key Words

shed
ship
shop
shut

dish
fish
wish

the
them
then

cloth
moth

Focus

A Match the words and pictures.
Write the words in your book.

> shed   fish   shop   ship   cloth   moth

1 sh_____

2 sh_____

3 sh_____

4 _____ sh

5 _____ th

6 _____ th

B Draw a picture to go with a **sh** word.

Copy these sentences.
Fill in the missing words.

1 shut or ship

The door is _____.

2 fish or wish

I have a gold _____.

3 think or thank

He said _____ you to his mum.

What am I?
Write the answers in your book.

cash   thin   brush   think   crash

1 I am a name for money.
2 I use my brain to do this.
3 You need me when you paint.
4 I happen when cars go too fast.
5 I am the opposite of thick.

Tricky Words
the   they   friend

ck
nk

Key Words

sack
neck
peck
kick
sock
duck

bank
tank

pink
sink

bunk
junk

Focus

A Add **ack** or **eck** to make these words.
Write the words in your book.

peck   neck   sack

1 s_____   **2** p_____   **3** n_____

B Add **ink** or **unk** to make these words.
Write the words in your book.

pink   bunk   junk

1 b_____   **2** p_____   **3** j_____

Copy these lists of **ck** and **nk** words.

kick   lock   duck   bank   pink
lick   rock   luck   tank   wink
sick   sock   suck   sank   sink

Tick the ones you can see in the picture.

What are they doing?
The words in the box will help you.

pick   wink   peck   sink   rock   kick

1 _____ ing   2 _____ ing   3 _____ ing

4 _____ ing   5 _____ ing   6 _____ ing

ch
tch

Wa**tch** that **ch**eeky **ch**imp!

Key Words

chat
chick
chin
chop

much
such

catch
hatch
match

ditch
pitch

hutch

Focus

Match the words and pictures.
Write the words in your book.

chin	chips	chimp
pitch	hutch	catch

1 ch _____

2 h _____

3 ch _____

4 p _____

5 ch _____

6 c _____

A Each of these sets of jumbled letters makes a **ch** word.
Can you sort them out?

1 atch   2 opch   3 ichmp

4 chus   5 ichwh   6 ichck

B Each of these sets of jumbled letters makes a **tch** word.
Can you sort them out?

1 tchhu   2 tchdi   3 tchca

Extension

A Lots of **ch** words have a tricky **t**.
Write the words from the Focus exercise in two lists, like this:

ch words   tch words
chips   hutch

B Write these sentences.
Choose the best word for each gap.

1 ditch   pitch

The ball was kicked off the _____ and into a _____.

2 match   catch

Her brilliant _____ won the _____.

3 hatch   hutch

We opened the _____ to clean the _____.

s
es

boy**s**

box**es**

bus**es**

seat**s**

Key Words

cats
girls
boys
dogs
windows

buses
boxes
foxes
bushes
brushes
classes
glasses

Focus

A Match a key word to each of these picture clues. Write the words in your book.

bushes	foxes	boys
girls	brushes	cats

1 b_____

2 c_____

3 g_____

4 f_____

5 b_____

6 br_____

B Write a sentence about one of the pictures.

14

We add **s** to some words when we are talking about more than one thing.

Write these words in your book, adding **s**. Like this:

1 cat   cats

1 cat	**2** pot
3 door	**4** table
5 snail	**6** tree
7 shed	**8** flower

Extension

If a word ends with **s**, **x**, **ch** or **sh** we add **es** when we are talking about more than one thing.

A Write these words in your book, adding **es**. Like this:

1 wish   wishes

1 wish	**2** class	**3** fox	**4** match
5 crash	**6** box	**7** torch	**8** catch

We also add **s** and **es** to verbs.

B Add **s** or **es** to these words.

1 dog	**2** like	**3** watch	**4** flash
5 kitten	**6** porch	**7** wash	**8** hutch

ing
ed
er

lick**ing**   lick**ed**   lick**er**

Key Words

kicking
licking
picking

bumping
jumping

talking
walking

resting
testing

Focus

A Match the words and pictures.
Write the words in your book.

talking	licking	jumping
kicking	picking	walking

1 p_____   2 k_____   3 l_____

4 j_____   5 w_____   6 t_____

B Write another **ing** word and draw a picture of it.

If something is **happening now**,
the action often ends with **ing.**

If something has **happened already**,
the action often ends with **ed.**

If somebody is doing something,
the noun often ends with **er.**

Copy this table of action words and their nouns.
Fill in the missing words.

happening now	already happened	noun
kicking	kicked	kicker
picking		
	licked	
		talker
	walked	

Extension

Match a word to each picture.

rubbing   sitting   dripping   cutting

1 _____   2 _____   3 _____   4 _____

What do you notice about these **ing** words?

UNIT 8

er est

long   long**er**   long**est**

Key Words

longer
longest

quicker
quickest

deeper
deepest

colder
coldest

smaller
smallest

taller
tallest

Focus

Match a key word to each of these picture clues.
Write the words in your book.

1 tall _____

2 t_____

3 t_____

4 small _____

5 s_____

6 s_____

7 quick _____

5 q_____

6 q_____

18

Extra

A Add **er** to each of the words in the box.
Write them neatly in your book, like this:

cold   colder

> cold   weak   fresh   light   rich   deep

B Write one of the words you have made
in a sentence.

Extension

A Add **est** to each of the words in the box.
Write them neatly in your book, like this:

cold   coldest

> cold   weak   fresh   light   rich   deep

B Write one of the words you have made
in a sentence.

ll ff
ss zz

Je**ss** ate flu**ff**,
And fi**zz**y je**ll**y,
Je**ss** went home
With a pain in her be**ll**y!

Key Words

off
puff
cliff

bell
tell
smell

fill
mill

dress
press
cross

buzz
fizz

Focus

A Match a key word to each of these picture clues.
Write the words in your book.

1 b_____   **2** dr_____   **3** cl_____

B What are they doing?
Write the words in your book.

1 b_____ing   **2** f_____ing   **3** dr_____ing

Extra

Copy these lists of **ll**, **ff**, **ss** and **zz** words.

hill	bell	huff	dress	buzz
mill	fell	puff	press	fizz
pill	yell	cliff	cross	jazz

Extension

To make the plural of most nouns we add **s**.
    one puff   two puff**s**

But if the word ends with **ss** we add **es**.
    one dress   two dress**es**

A Write the plural of these words.

1 hill   2 bell

3 pill   4 cliff

5 huff   6 cuff

B Write the plural of these words.

1 mess   2 press

3 grass   4 cross

5 buzz   6 fizz

a-e
ai ay

A sn**ai**l **a**t**e** the fl**a**k**e** on my birthd**ay** c**a**k**e**!

Key Words

came
game
same
blame
flame

tail
nail
snail

ray
tray
stray
play

day
today

Focus

Match the words and pictures.
Write the words in your book.

cake   rake   wave   case   gate   lake

1 r_____

2 c_____

3 l_____

4 c_____

5 w_____

6 g_____

Copy these lists of rhyming **ai** words.
Tick the ones you can see in the picture.

rail	raid	train
snail	maid	plain
mail	paid	Spain
sail	afraid	chain

Extension

What am I?
Write the answers in your book.

bay   clay   hay   day   tray   today

1 I am found at the seaside.
2 I'm the opposite of night.
3 I'm dried grass.
4 I'm used to make pots.
5 I carry cups and plates.
6 I'm the day before tomorrow.

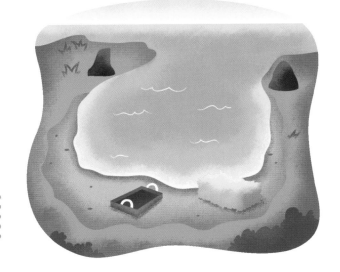

Tricky Words
today   said   says

ee ea
ie e-e

Key Words

bee
see
tree

feed
seed
weed

sea
tea
pea

eat
meat
clean

these
chief

Can you s**ee** the b**ee**s in the tr**ee**?

They make the honey I **ea**t for my t**ea**.

Focus

Find a key word to match each picture.
Write the words in your book.

1 b_____   2 t_____   3 s_____

4 s_____   5 e_____   6 p_____

Extra

Find seven **ie** and **e-e** words hidden in this puzzle.

k	g	g	f	g	c	s	n	t
x	l	r	i	b	s	t	q	h
b	r	i	e	f	l	h	e	e
q	s	e	l	k	w	i	f	s
z	x	f	d	t	h	e	m	e
c	h	i	e	f	d	f	z	i

Sometimes **ie** and **e-e** can sound like **ee** and **ea**, like chief, these.

Extension

What am I doing?
The words in the box will give you a clue.

weed	teach	bleed	scream
meet	sleep	eat	clean

Adding **ing** means it is happening now.

1 _____ ing   2 _____ ing   3 _____ ing   4 _____ ing

5 _____ ing   6 _____ ing   7 _____ ing   8 _____ ing

Tricky Words
be   he   me   we   she   these

i-e ie
igh y

I l**i**k**e** to be safe in m**y** home at n**igh**t.

Key Words

bike
like

dive
five

tie
pie

high
fight
light
might
bright

my
cry
fly
shy
why

Focus

Match a key word to each of these picture clues.
Write the words in your book.

1 b _____

2 d _____

3 f _____

4 t _____

5 p _____

6 l _____

7 s _____

8 c _____

9 f _____

What am I doing?
Find a word in the box to match each picture.

> crying   drying   frying
> flying   fighting   lighting

1 l_____ 2 fr_____ 3 fl_____

4 f_____ 5 cr_____ 6 dr_____

Extension

> bit   sit   kit   pin   fin   pip   rip

A Copy the words in the box.
Now add a **'magic' e** to the end of each one,
like this:

bit   bite

B Which of your new words match these clues?
Write the answers in your book.

1 It flies in the sky.
2 This is the place where builders work.
3 To eat you do this.
4 It carries water to a tap.
5 Fruit like this is ready to eat.

> **Tricky Words**
> live   give

oa o-e
oe ow

Green t**oa**d
    Black r**oa**d
Red lorry
    Large l**oa**d
Green r**oa**d
    Flat t**oa**d.

Constance Milburn

Key Words

boat
coat

load
road
toad

smoke
choke
alone
stone

snow
blow
show

toes
goes

Focus

A Look at the poem again.
Copy the words with the **oa** pattern.

B Find two **o-e** words and two **ow** words
in this picture.
Write them neatly in your book.

grow	boast	flow	broke	coast	toes	blow
smoke	toast	throw	choke	roast	spoke	goes

Sort the words in the box into rhyming families,
like this:

oke words	**oast** words	**oes** words	**ow** words
broke	boast	goes	blow

Extension

These words have the **oa** sound but do not have
oa, **o-e** or **ow**.

| most | post | host | almost |

Match a word from the box with each clue.

1 letters and parcels
2 nearly all
3 nearly
4 looks after visitors

Tricky Words

go   no   so

oo
u-e
ue ew

Key Words

zoo

boot
hoot

moon
soon

room
zoom

new
chew
screw

June
tune

blue
glue

Focus

Match the words and pictures.
Write the words in your book.

zoo   boot   moon   spoon   food   roof

1 b_____

2 sp_____

3 r_____

4 z_____

5 m_____

6 f_____

Extra

Copy and finish these word sums.

1 m + oo   = moo
2 br + oo + m =
3 f + ew   =
4 st + ew   =
5 J + u + n + e =
6 c + u + b + e =
7 gl + ue   =
8 tr + ue   =
9 c + oo + t   =
10 st + oo + p =

Extension

new	root	glue	few	clue	hoot
dew	shoot	blue	chew	true	scoot

Sort the words in the box into letter pattern families, like this:

ew words	**oot** words	**ue** words
new	root	glue

Check-up 1

Write a word to match the picture.

1 c_____ 2 h_____ 3 f_____ 4 d_____

5 ch_____ 6 h_____ 7 b_____ 8 l_____

9 d_____ 10 s_____ 11 b_____ 12 f_____

13 b_____ 14 m_____ 15 s_____ 16 b_____

Extension

Write two words that rhyme with:

1 park   2 cry   3 dish   4 mess   5 toad